THE FINANCIAL FREEDOM FORMULA

A STEP-BY-STEP GUIDE TO FINANCIAL INDEPENDENCE

JOY DANIELS

Copyright © 2024 by JOY DANIELS

TABLE OF CONTENT

INTRODUCTION

Welcome to "The Financial Freedom Formula: A Step-by-Step Guide to Financial Independence," your comprehensive roadmap to achieving true financial freedom. In a world where economic landscapes are constantly evolving, this book serves as your trustworthy guide to navigate the complexities of personal finance and embark on a transformative journey towards lasting financial independence.

In these pages, we unravel the mysteries surrounding wealth creation and provide you with a practical blueprint to break free from financial constraints. The Financial Freedom Formula is not just a book; it's a powerful tool designed to empower you with the knowledge and strategies needed to take control of your financial destiny.

This book goes beyond conventional financial advice, offering a step-by-step approach that demystifies the process of building wealth. Whether you're just starting on your financial journey or seeking to enhance your current financial standing, this guide caters to all levels of expertise. We believe that financial freedom is not an exclusive privilege but a goal attainable by anyone with the right mindset and tools.

Each chapter is crafted with precision, covering topics such as budgeting, investing, debt management, and income generation. You'll discover practical tips, real-life examples, and actionable advice to implement immediately. From setting realistic financial goals to creating sustainable income streams, The Financial Freedom Formula equips you with the tools to make informed decisions and build a solid foundation for your financial future.

Embrace this opportunity to transform your relationship with money, gain control over your finances, and ultimately achieve the freedom to live life on your terms. The Financial Freedom Formula is not just a book; it's your guide to unlocking the doors to financial independence and realizing your dreams. Get ready to embark on a life-changing journey towards a brighter, more financially secure future.

CHAPTER 1: UNDERSTANDING FINANCIAL FREEDOM

Welcome to the opening chapter of "The Financial Freedom Formula: A Step-by-Step Guide to Financial Independence." In this crucial section, we embark on a journey of self-discovery and financial enlightenment, delving into the fundamental concept of understanding financial freedom. To navigate the complex realm of personal finance, it is imperative to grasp the essence of what financial freedom truly means and why it holds the key to unlocking a life of abundance.

In "Understanding Financial Freedom," we start by defining the term in a way that goes beyond mere monetary wealth. We explore the profound impact that financial independence can have on various aspects of your life, from reducing stress and anxiety to enabling you to pursue your passions and dreams. It's not just about accumulating wealth; it's about gaining control over your financial destiny and shaping a future that aligns with your values and aspirations.

This chapter serves as the cornerstone for the entire book, laying the groundwork for a transformative journey toward lasting financial empowerment. We delve into the interconnectedness of financial decisions, personal values, and life goals, emphasizing that true financial freedom is a holistic pursuit that extends beyond dollars and cents.

As we embark on this exploration, you'll gain insights into assessing your current financial situation, setting meaningful goals, and understanding the profound impact that achieving financial freedom can have on your overall well-being. Prepare to challenge conventional notions and embrace a new perspective on money—one that propels you toward a future where your financial decisions align with your deepest desires.

Join us in unravelling the mysteries of financial freedom and discover the first steps towards reshaping your financial narrative. Let's begin this transformative journey together.

-Financial Freedom

Financial freedom is a state of being where an individual can make choices about their life without being overly constrained by financial concerns. It is more than just accumulating wealth; it involves achieving a level of financial stability and independence that allows individuals to live life on their own terms. This comprehensive exploration will delve into the various dimensions of financial freedom, its significance, and the practical steps one can take to attain it.

1. Definition and Dimensions:

Financial freedom is the capacity to meet one's financial needs and goals, providing a sense of security and control over one's financial future. It encompasses multiple dimensions, including freedom from debt, the ability to cover living expenses comfortably, and having surplus resources for investments and personal pursuits.

2. Breaking down Barriers:

This section addresses the common barriers that hinder financial freedom, such as debt, lack of savings, and limited income streams. Strategies for overcoming these obstacles, like debt repayment plans and budgeting techniques, are explored to empower individuals to take charge of their financial destinies.

3. Building a Foundation:

Financial freedom necessitates a solid foundation. Chapters on budgeting, emergency funds, and goal setting are vital components in constructing this groundwork. Readers will learn practical techniques for creating and sticking to a budget, establishing emergency funds for unforeseen circumstances, and setting achievable financial goals.

4. **Investing for Wealth Creation:**

One key avenue towards financial freedom is strategic investing. This section demystifies investment concepts, exploring various asset classes like stocks, bonds, and real estate. It provides readers with the knowledge to create a diversified investment portfolio tailored to their risk tolerance and financial objectives.

5. **Sustainable Income Streams:**

A crucial aspect of financial freedom is the creation of multiple and sustainable income streams. This chapter delves into active and passive income sources, including side hustles, investments, and entrepreneurship. Readers will learn how to leverage their skills and assets to generate income beyond traditional employment.

6. **Navigating Life Transitions:**

Life is dynamic, and financial freedom requires adaptability. This section addresses how to navigate major life transitions such as job changes, starting a family, or retirement. Strategies for adjusting financial plans and maintaining freedom through various life stages are explored.

7. beyond Finances:

Financial freedom extends beyond monetary aspects. This chapter explores the psychological and emotional dimensions, emphasizing the importance of aligning financial decisions with personal values and goals. It encourages readers to envision a life where financial freedom contributes to overall well-being and fulfilment.

In essence, this comprehensive exploration of financial freedom provides readers with the tools, knowledge, and mindset necessary to embark on a transformative journey towards a more liberated and purpose-driven financial life. By understanding the intricacies of financial freedom, individuals can transcend the limitations of financial stress and chart a course towards a more empowered and fulfilling future.

- The Importance of Financial Independence

Financial independence is a state where an individual has sufficient financial resources to sustain their desired lifestyle without being reliant on external sources of income. This concept holds immense importance in various aspects of an individual's life, influencing not only their financial well-being but also their overall sense of freedom and fulfilment. This comprehensive analysis explores the multifaceted significance of financial independence.

1. Autonomy and Decision-Making:

Financial independence empowers individuals to make decisions based on personal preferences rather than financial constraints. Whether it's choosing a career path, pursuing further education, or deciding on major life events, financial independence provides the freedom to align choices with individual values and aspirations.

2. Reduced Stress and Improved Mental Well-Being:

Financial stress is a prevalent issue that affects mental health. Financial independence alleviates this stress, promoting mental well-being. Individuals can experience reduced anxiety and an enhanced sense of security, fostering a positive mindset and better overall mental health.

3. Flexibility and Adaptability:

Financially independent individuals are better equipped to navigate life's uncertainties. They have the flexibility to adapt to unexpected events, such as job loss or health crises, without facing immediate financial crises. This adaptability contributes to resilience and a more confident approach to life's challenges.

4. Opportunities for Personal Growth:

Financial independence creates opportunities for personal development and growth. Whether it's pursuing hobbies, investing in education, or travelling, individuals can dedicate time and resources to activities that contribute to personal fulfilment and self-improvement.

5. Retirement Planning and Long-Term Security:

Financial independence plays a pivotal role in retirement planning. Individuals who achieve financial independence can retire comfortably and maintain their desired lifestyle without being solely reliant on social security or pensions. This long-term security enhances the quality of life during retirement.

6. Entrepreneurial Pursuits:

Financial independence provides a launchpad for entrepreneurial endeavors. Individuals with financial stability are more likely to take calculated risks, start their businesses, and pursue innovative ventures without the fear of immediate financial failure.

7. Generational Impact:

Financial independence extends its impact across generations. Families with a legacy of financial independence can provide better opportunities for their children and grandchildren, breaking the cycle of financial dependence and fostering a culture of financial responsibility.

8. Philanthropy and Social Impact:

Financially independent individuals can contribute to charitable causes and make a positive impact on society. Whether through donations, volunteer work, or supporting social initiatives, financial independence enables individuals to actively participate in making a difference in the world.

9. Enhanced Relationship Dynamics:

Financial strain is a common source of tension in relationships. Financial independence allows individuals to contribute to shared financial goals, fostering healthier relationships. Couples can make joint decisions without the burden of financial disparities.

In conclusion, the importance of financial independence transcends mere monetary considerations. It is a catalyst for personal freedom, mental well-being, and the pursuit of a fulfilling life. By attaining financial independence, individuals can shape their destinies, contribute to societal well-being, and enjoy a sense of autonomy that permeates every aspect of their lives.

- Assessing Your Current Financial Situation

Assessing your current financial situation is a crucial first step towards achieving financial independence. This process involves a comprehensive evaluation of your income, expenses, assets, and liabilities to gain a clear understanding of your financial health. Here's a step-by-step guide to navigating this important aspect of financial management:

1. Gather Financial Documents:

Begin by collecting all relevant financial documents, including pay stubs, bank statements, credit card statements, investment statements, tax returns, and any other records that provide insights into your financial position.

2. Calculate Net Worth:

Determine your net worth by subtracting your liabilities (debts) from your assets. Assets include savings, investments, properties, and valuable possessions, while liabilities encompass loans, credit card debt, and other obligations. A positive net worth indicates financial health.

3. Analyze Income and Expenses:

Examine your sources of income and create a detailed list of monthly expenses. Categorize expenses into fixed (mortgage, rent, utilities) and variable (groceries, entertainment). Understanding the balance between income and expenses is crucial for budgeting and identifying areas for potential savings.

4. Evaluate Debt Levels:

Assess your debt situation by listing all outstanding debts along with their interest rates. Prioritize high-interest debts for faster repayment. Understanding your debt load is essential for formulating effective debt management strategies.

5. Review Credit Score:

Obtain and review your credit report to assess your credit score. A good credit score is essential for favorable interest rates on loans and financial flexibility. Address any discrepancies and work on improving your credit if needed.

6. Examine Emergency Fund:

Evaluate the adequacy of your emergency fund. A well-funded emergency fund provides a financial cushion during unexpected expenses or periods of

income disruption. Aim for three to six months'
worth of living expenses in your emergency fund.

7. Assess Investment Portfolio:

Review your investment holdings and assess their
performance. Ensure that your investment strategy
aligns with your financial goals, risk tolerance, and
time horizon. Consider diversification to spread risk
across different asset classes.

8. Insurance Coverage:

Evaluate your insurance coverage, including
health, life, property, and auto insurance. Ensure
that coverage meets your current needs and consider
adjustments based on changes in your life
circumstances.

9. Consider Tax Implications:

Assess your tax situation, considering potential
deductions and credits. Optimize your tax strategy

to minimize liabilities and maximize savings. Consult with a tax professional if necessary.

10. Identify Financial Goals:

Clearly define short-term and long-term financial goals. Whether it's saving for a home, education, or retirement, having well-defined goals provides direction for your financial decisions.

11. Budget Creation:

Develop a realistic budget based on your income, expenses, and financial goals. A budget serves as a roadmap for managing your finances and helps you allocate resources efficiently.

12. Regular Monitoring and Adjustments:

Financial assessment is not a one-time task. Regularly monitor your financial situation, track progress toward goals, and make adjustments as needed. Life circumstances change, and your financial plan should adapt accordingly.

In conclusion, assessing your current financial situation is a dynamic and ongoing process that lays the foundation for effective financial management. It empowers you to make informed decisions, set realistic goals, and embark on a path towards financial independence. Regularly revisiting and updating this assessment ensures that your financial strategies remain aligned with your evolving needs and aspirations.

CHAPTER 2: CRAFTING YOUR FINANCIAL BLUEPRINT

Welcome to the pivotal chapter in your journey towards financial independence – "Crafting Your Financial Blueprint." Just as a skilled artisan meticulously plans and designs their masterpiece, this chapter invites you to intricately design the blueprint for your financial future. It's a roadmap tailored to your unique goals, aspirations, and circumstances, guiding you towards the financial freedom you seek.

Crafting a financial blueprint is more than just creating a budget; it's about architecting a comprehensive plan that aligns with your values, dreams, and the life you envision. In the following pages, we delve into the art and science of financial planning, providing you with the tools and insights necessary to shape a financial framework that not only supports your present needs but also paves the way for future prosperity.

This chapter unfolds in a step-by-step fashion, leading you through the essential elements of crafting a robust financial blueprint. From setting realistic financial goals to creating a personalized budget, we explore the intricacies of managing income, expenses, and savings. This isn't a one-size-fits-all approach; instead, it's a customizable guide to help you sculpt a financial strategy that resonates with your unique circumstances.

As we embark on this journey, envision your financial blueprint as a dynamic document that evolves with your life. It's a tool that adapts to changes, accommodates new goals, and remains resilient in the face of unforeseen circumstances. The act of crafting this blueprint is an empowering exercise, putting you in control of your financial narrative and paving the way for a future filled with financial confidence and security.

So, let's pick up our metaphorical pens and begin crafting. Let's sketch out the lines and contours of a financial plan that reflects your dreams and aspirations. Through thoughtful consideration and strategic planning, we'll lay the foundation for a secure and prosperous financial future. The canvas is yours, and this chapter is your guide to creating a financial masterpiece uniquely yours.

- Setting Realistic Financial Goals

Setting realistic financial goals is a fundamental step on the path to financial independence. Thoughtfully defined objectives provide direction, motivation, and a clear framework for financial decision-making. In this comprehensive guide, we explore the process of establishing realistic financial goals to help you navigate your journey toward a secure and prosperous financial future.

1. Self-Reflection and Prioritization:

Begin by reflecting on your values, aspirations, and life priorities. Consider short-term and long-term goals, both financial and non-financial. Prioritize these goals based on their importance to you and their alignment with your vision for the future.

2. Specificity and Clarity:

Make your goals specific and clear. Instead of a vague objective like "save money," specify the amount and the purpose, such as "save $5,000 for an emergency fund." Clarity in your goals enhances focus and provides a measurable target.

3. Measurable Targets:

Establish measurable criteria for your goals. This could involve setting a specific dollar amount, percentage of income, or a timeline for achievement. Measurable targets allow you to track progress and celebrate milestones along the way.

4. **Achievability and Realism:**

Goals should be challenging yet attainable. Assess your current financial situation, taking into account income, expenses, and other obligations. Setting overly ambitious goals can lead to frustration, while overly modest goals may lack the motivation needed for progress.

5. **Time-Bound Objectives:**

Attach a timeframe to each goal. Whether it's short-term goals like paying off credit card debt in six months or long-term goals like saving for a down payment in five years, a time frame adds a sense of urgency and provides a structured timeline for action.

6. **Categorization of Goals:**

Categorize your goals based on their nature. Common categories include short-term (within a year), mid-term (1-5 years), and long-term (5+ years). This helps in creating a balanced and well-rounded financial plan.

7. **Prioritization of Goals:**

Once you've identified and categorized your goals, prioritize them based on urgency and importance. Consider which goals need immediate attention and which can be pursued over a more extended period. This prioritization helps in allocating resources efficiently.

8. **Alignment with Values:**

Ensure that your financial goals align with your core values. Goals that resonate with your values are more likely to be pursued with dedication and commitment. This alignment adds a sense of purpose to your financial journey.

9. **Regular Review and Adjustments:**

Financial goals are not set in stone. Regularly review and reassess your goals, considering changes in your life circumstances, income, and priorities. Adjustments may be necessary to keep your goals relevant and achievable.

10. Breaking Down Larger Goals:

If you have substantial long-term goals, break them down into smaller, more manageable milestones. This makes the overall objective less overwhelming and allows for incremental progress.

11. Incorporating Flexibility:

Recognize that life is dynamic, and unexpected events may impact your goals. Build flexibility into your plan to adapt to changing circumstances while staying focused on your overarching objectives.

12. Celebrate Achievements:

Acknowledge and celebrate your successes along the way. Whether it's reaching a savings milestone or paying off debt, recognizing achievements reinforces positive financial habits and motivates continued progress.

In conclusion, the process of setting realistic financial goals is a thoughtful and dynamic exercise that forms the backbone of your financial plan. By following these steps, you create a roadmap that aligns with your values, motivates action, and propels you towards financial success. Remember, your financial goals are personal, and crafting them with care sets the stage for a fulfilling and secure financial future.

- Creating a Personalized Budget

Crafting a personalized budget is a fundamental and empowering step toward achieving financial independence. A well-designed budget serves as a roadmap for managing income, controlling expenses, and directing resources toward your financial goals. In this comprehensive guide, we explore the process of creating a personalized budget to help you gain control over your finances and work towards a secure financial future.

1. Gather Financial Information:

Begin by collecting detailed information about your income, including salary, bonuses, and other sources. Additionally, compile a comprehensive list of your expenses, covering both fixed (e.g., rent, mortgage) and variable (e.g., groceries, entertainment) costs.

2. Categorize Income and Expenses:

Categorize your income and expenses into clear and distinct categories. This categorization provides a structured overview of where your money comes from and where it goes. Common categories include housing, transportation, utilities, groceries, debt payments, and discretionary spending.

3. Determine Fixed and Variable Expenses:

Differentiate between fixed and variable expenses. Fixed expenses remain relatively constant each month, while variable expenses may fluctuate. Understanding this distinction helps in identifying areas where you have more control over spending.

4. Calculate Net Income:

Subtract your total expenses from your total income to determine your net income. This figure represents the amount of money available for saving, investing, and achieving financial goals. If your expenses exceed your income, adjustments may be needed.

5. Identify Non-Monthly Expenses:

Consider non-monthly expenses, such as annual insurance premiums or quarterly taxes. Allocate a portion of your monthly budget to these irregular expenses, ensuring that you're prepared for them when they occur.

6. Establish Emergency Fund Allocation:

Allocate a portion of your budget to building and maintaining an emergency fund. This financial cushion serves as a buffer for unexpected expenses and provides peace of mind in times of financial uncertainty.

7. Set Savings Goals:

Define specific savings goals within your budget, whether it's for a vacation, a down payment on a house, or retirement. Allocate a portion of your income to these goals, treating them as non-negotiable components of your budget.

8. Review and Prioritize Expenses:

Review your variable expenses and prioritize them based on necessity and personal values. This step allows you to identify areas where you can potentially cut back without sacrificing essential needs or values.

9. Implement Budgeting Tools:

Leverage technology and budgeting apps to streamline the process. Many apps categorize expenses automatically, provide insights into spending patterns, and offer alerts when approaching budget limits.

10. Track and Monitor Spending:

Regularly track your spending against the budget to ensure adherence. Monitoring your financial habits allows for quick adjustments and reinforces positive spending behaviors.

11. Make Adjustments as Needed:

Be flexible and open to making adjustments as circumstances change. Life is dynamic, and your budget should adapt to new income levels, expenses, and financial goals.

12. Review Regularly:

Establish a routine for budget reviews. Regularly assess your financial situation, reassess your goals, and make necessary adjustments to keep your budget aligned with your evolving priorities.

13. Seek Professional Guidance:

If needed, seek advice from financial professionals. A financial advisor can provide insights, help refine your budgeting strategies, and offer guidance on optimizing your financial plan.

In conclusion, creating a personalized budget is a dynamic and ongoing process that empowers you to take control of your financial destiny. By following these steps and embracing the flexibility to adapt, your budget becomes a powerful tool for achieving financial goals, managing resources effectively, and ultimately realizing financial independence. Remember, your budget is a reflection of your priorities, and by crafting it with care, you pave the way for a more secure and prosperous future.

- Building Emergency Funds for Stability

Building an emergency fund is a crucial step in achieving financial stability. This financial cushion provides a safety net, helping you navigate unexpected expenses, income disruptions, or unforeseen emergencies without derailing your overall financial plan. In this comprehensive guide, we explore the process of building emergency funds to enhance your financial resilience and peace of mind.

1. **Assess Your Financial Situation:**

Begin by evaluating your current financial status, including income, expenses, and outstanding debts. Understanding your baseline financial health is essential for determining the size of the emergency fund needed.

2. **Define Your Emergency Fund Goal:**

Establish a specific goal for your emergency fund. Financial experts often recommend saving three to six months' worth of living expenses. However, the ideal amount depends on individual circumstances, such as job stability, family size, and risk tolerance.

3. **Start Small, Be Consistent:**

If saving a substantial amount seems daunting, start small but be consistent. Set achievable monthly savings goals and gradually increase the amount as your financial situation improves. The key is to establish a habit of saving regularly.

4. Create a Separate Account:

Open a separate savings account dedicated solely to your emergency fund. Keeping the fund separate from your regular spending account reduces the temptation to dip into it for non-emergencies.

5. Automate Savings:

Set up automatic transfers from your primary account to your emergency fund. Automation ensures that a portion of your income is consistently allocated to your emergency fund, fostering disciplined savings.

6. Prioritize High-Interest Debt Repayment:

If you have high-interest debts, consider prioritizing debt repayment alongside building your emergency fund. Reducing high-interest debts frees up more resources for savings in the long run.

7. Adjust Based on Life Changes:

Life circumstances change, and so should your emergency fund goal. Reevaluate your fund size when major life changes occur, such as marriage, the birth of a child, or a new job. Adjust your savings targets accordingly.

8. Consider Non-Monthly Expenses:

Factor in non-monthly expenses when determining your emergency fund goal. This includes irregular expenses like insurance premiums or annual taxes. Having funds set aside for these items contributes to comprehensive financial stability.

9. Avoid Unnecessary Risks:

While the goal is to build an emergency fund, avoid unnecessary risks that could jeopardize your financial well-being. Ensure that you have adequate insurance coverage for potential risks such as health, property, and life.

10. Replenish After Utilization:

In the event of an emergency, use the funds as intended. Once the emergency is resolved, prioritize replenishing the fund to its target amount. This ensures the fund is ready for the next unexpected situation.

11. Reassess Fund Size Over Time:

As your financial situation evolves, reassess the size of your emergency fund. Factors such as changes in income, family size, or overall expenses may necessitate adjustments to your savings goals.

12. Educate Family Members:

If applicable, ensure that family members are aware of the purpose of the emergency fund and the importance of not using it for non-emergencies. Open communication promotes a collective understanding and commitment to financial stability.

13. Celebrate Milestones:

Acknowledge and celebrate milestones in your emergency fund journey. Whether it's reaching a certain savings target or successfully weathering an unexpected expense, recognizing achievements reinforces positive financial habits.

14. Revisit Fund Allocation:

Periodically review the allocation of your emergency fund. Evaluate whether the current distribution between liquid assets and investments aligns with your risk tolerance and liquidity needs.

In conclusion, building emergency funds is an ongoing process that requires discipline, consistency, and adaptability. By following these steps and making emergency fund savings a priority, you fortify your financial stability, enabling you to face uncertainties with confidence and resilience. Remember, an emergency fund is an investment in your financial well-being, providing the stability needed to pursue long-term financial goals.

CHAPTER 3:
MASTERING THE ART OF INVESTING

Welcome to the gateway of financial empowerment and wealth creation – "Mastering the Art of Investing." In this pivotal chapter, we embark on a journey that demystifies the complexities of investing, providing you with the knowledge and tools to navigate the financial markets with confidence and acumen. Investing is not just about growing wealth; it's a strategic endeavor that, when approached with understanding and skill, can unlock the doors to financial freedom.

In "Mastering the Art of Investing," we delve into the principles, strategies, and nuances of this multifaceted realm. Whether you're a novice seeking to build a foundation or a seasoned investor aiming to refine your approach, this chapter is designed to cater to all levels of expertise. We explore the various asset classes, risk management techniques, and the psychology behind successful investing.

This isn't just a guide to picking stocks or bonds; it's a comprehensive exploration of the mindset and skills needed to make informed investment decisions. As we venture into the intricacies of the financial markets, you'll gain insights into building a diversified portfolio, understanding market trends, and developing a long-term investment strategy that aligns with your financial goals.

Investing is an art that combines knowledge, discipline, and adaptability. In the following pages, we break down the barriers that often intimidate aspiring investors, providing you with a roadmap to navigate the ever-changing landscape of the financial world. From the basics of investment terminology to advanced strategies for wealth creation, this chapter is your compass in the vast and dynamic universe of investing.

So, whether you're looking to secure your financial future, generate passive income, or pursue ambitious wealth-building goals, "Mastering the Art of Investing" is your guide to unlocking the potential of your money. Get ready to delve into the artistry of investment, where informed decisions and strategic choices sculpt a future of financial prosperity and independence. The canvas is yours, and this chapter is your brushstroke towards mastering the art of investing.

- Investing Principles

Investing is a powerful tool for building wealth and achieving financial goals. To navigate the complex world of investing successfully, it's crucial to understand and apply fundamental investing principles. These principles serve as guiding lights, shaping strategies, and influencing decisions. In this comprehensive guide, we explore the key investing principles that form the bedrock of a successful and sustainable investment approach.

1. **Set Clear Goals:**

Define your investment objectives. Whether it's saving for retirement, funding education, or building wealth, having clear goals helps tailor your investment strategy to meet specific financial milestones.

2. **Understand Risk and Reward:**

Recognize the relationship between risk and reward. Investments with higher potential returns often come with higher risks. Assess your risk tolerance and align investments with your comfort level to strike a balance between risk and potential reward.

3. **Diversification:**

"Don't put all your eggs in one basket." Diversification involves spreading investments across different asset classes (stocks, bonds, real estate) to reduce risk. A well-diversified portfolio can provide stability during market fluctuations.

4. **Time in the Market, Not Timing the Market:**

Attempting to time the market—predicting when to buy or sell based on short-term trends—is challenging and often counterproductive. Focus on a long-term investment horizon, benefiting from the compounding of returns over time.

5. **Invest According to Your Risk Tolerance:**

Your risk tolerance is influenced by factors like age, financial goals, and personal comfort with market fluctuations. Invest in assets that align with your risk tolerance to ensure a more stable and less stressful investment journey.

6. **Continuous Learning:**

Stay informed about market trends, economic indicators, and investment opportunities. The financial landscape evolves, and ongoing education equips you with the knowledge to make informed investment decisions.

7. Costs Matter:

Be mindful of investment costs, including fees and expenses. High fees can erode returns over time. Opt for cost-effective investment vehicles and consider low-cost index funds or exchange-traded funds (ETFs).

8. Emergency Fund:

Before diving into investing, ensure you have an emergency fund. This fund provides a financial safety net, reducing the need to liquidate investments in times of unexpected expenses or income disruptions.

9. Long-Term Perspective:

Investing is a marathon, not a sprint. Maintain a long-term perspective, resisting the urge to react to short-term market fluctuations. Consistency and patience are essential for enduring success.

10. Stay Disciplined:

Develop and stick to an investment plan. Emotional reactions to market volatility can lead to impulsive decisions. A disciplined approach involves periodic reviews and adjustments based on your long-term goals.

11. Reinvest Dividends:

Reinvesting dividends can significantly enhance the power of compounding. Instead of receiving dividend payouts, reinvest them to purchase additional shares, accelerating the growth of your investment.

12. Regular Portfolio Rebalancing:

Periodically rebalance your portfolio to maintain the desired asset allocation. Market fluctuations can cause deviations from the original allocation, and rebalancing ensures alignment with your risk tolerance and goals.

13. Seek Professional Advice:

Consider seeking advice from financial professionals, especially for complex financial situations or specialized investment strategies. A financial advisor can provide personalized guidance tailored to your unique circumstances.

14. **Review and Adjust:**

Regularly review your investment portfolio and financial goals. Life circumstances change, and adjustments may be necessary. Periodic assessments ensure your investments remain aligned with your evolving needs and aspirations.

By adhering to these investing principles, you build a solid foundation for a successful and resilient investment strategy. Remember, investing is a journey that requires commitment, education, and adaptability. With these principles as your guide, you can navigate the complexities of the financial markets with confidence and work towards achieving your long-term financial goals.

- Types of Investments: Stocks, Bonds, Real Estate, and More

Investing is a dynamic field with a plethora of options catering to various risk appetites, goals, and preferences. Understanding the different types of investments is crucial for building a diversified and well-balanced portfolio. In this comprehensive guide, we explore some key investment types, including stocks, bonds, real estate, and other assets.

1. **Stocks:**

   - **Description:** Stocks, also known as equities, represent ownership in a company. When you buy shares of a company's stock, you become a partial owner and may benefit from its success through capital appreciation and dividends.

- **Risk and Reward:** Stocks are considered higher-risk, higher-reward investments. Prices can be volatile, but historically, they have provided significant returns over the long term.

2. **Bonds:**

   - Description: Bonds are debt securities issued by governments, municipalities, or corporations. When you purchase a bond, you are essentially lending money to the issuer in exchange for periodic interest payments and the return of the principal amount at maturity.

   - **Risk and Reward:** Bonds are generally considered lower-risk investments compared to stocks. They provide regular income through interest payments and are often used for capital preservation.

3. **Real Estate:**

   - Description: Real estate investments involve buying and owning physical properties, such as residential or commercial real estate, to generate rental income or capital appreciation.

  - **Risk and Reward:** Real estate can offer a steady income stream through rent and potential appreciation. However, it requires substantial capital and property values can fluctuate based on economic conditions.

4. Mutual Funds:

  - **Description:** Mutual funds pool money from multiple investors to invest in a diversified portfolio of stocks, bonds, or other securities. They are managed by professional fund managers.

  - **Risk and Reward:** Mutual funds provide diversification and professional management. However, fees and expenses can impact overall returns.

5. Exchange-Traded Funds (ETFs):

  - Description: ETFs are similar to mutual funds but trade on stock exchanges like individual stocks. They often track an index and offer diversification.

- Risk and Reward: ETFs combine the diversification of mutual funds with the flexibility of individual stocks. They are generally cost-effective and liquid.

6. Certificates of Deposit (CDs):

- **Description:** CDs are time deposits offered by banks with fixed interest rates and maturity dates. Investors receive their principal and interest upon maturity.

- **Risk and Reward:** CDs are low-risk, providing a fixed return. However, liquidity is limited until the maturity date, and interest rates may not keep pace with inflation.

7. Precious Metals:

- **Description:** Investments in precious metals like gold and silver serve as a hedge against inflation and economic uncertainty. Investors can buy physical metals or invest in related financial products.

- **Risk and Reward:** Precious metals are often considered a safe-haven investment. They can provide diversification, but their value is influenced by market sentiment.

8. Cryptocurrencies:

- **Description:** Cryptocurrencies like Bitcoin and Ethereum are digital or virtual currencies using cryptography for security. They operate on decentralized blockchain technology.

- **Risk and Reward:** Cryptocurrencies are highly volatile and speculative. They offer the potential for high returns but come with significant risk due to regulatory uncertainties and market fluctuations.

9. Collectibles:

- **Description:** Collectibles, such as art, vintage cars, or rare stamps, can be considered alternative investments. Their value is often appreciated based on rarity and demand.

- **Risk and Reward**: Collectibles can offer unique returns, but their value is subjective and influenced by market trends and individual preferences.

10. Peer-to-Peer Lending:

- **Description:** Peer-to-peer lending platforms connect borrowers with individual lenders. Investors can earn interest by lending money directly to individuals or small businesses.

- **Risk and Reward:** While P2P lending provides an alternative income stream, it involves credit risk and borrower default. Investors should diversify across multiple loans.

11. Options and Derivatives:

- **Description:** Options and derivatives are financial instruments derived from underlying assets. They provide investors with the right to buy or sell assets at predetermined prices.

- **Risk and Reward:** Options and derivatives are complex and carry high risk. They are often used for hedging or speculative purposes and require a deep understanding of the market.

Understanding the characteristics, risks, and potential rewards of these investment types is essential for constructing a diversified and well-aligned investment portfolio. Depending on your financial goals, risk tolerance, and investment horizon, a combination of these assets can contribute to a robust and tailored investment strategy. Always seek professional advice and conduct thorough research before making investment decisions.

- Creating a Diversified Investment Portfolio

Creating a diversified investment portfolio is a cornerstone of sound financial management.

Diversification involves spreading your investments across various asset classes to manage risk and optimize returns. In this comprehensive guide, we explore the step-by-step process of building a diversified investment portfolio tailored to your financial goals, risk tolerance, and time horizon.

1. Set Clear Investment Goals:

Define your investment objectives. Whether you're saving for retirement, a home purchase, or education, clear goals guide the selection of assets in your portfolio.

2. Understand Risk Tolerance:

Assess your risk tolerance, considering factors such as age, financial situation, and comfort with market fluctuations. Your risk tolerance influences the mix of assets in your portfolio.

3. Identify Asset Classes:

Recognize different asset classes, including stocks, bonds, real estate, and cash equivalents.

Each asset class has unique risk and return characteristics, providing diversification benefits.

4. Determine Asset Allocation:

Allocate your investment capital among different asset classes based on your risk tolerance and investment goals. Common allocations include a combination of stocks and bonds.

5. Consider Geographic and Sector Diversification:

Broaden diversification by considering geographic and sector allocations. Invest in assets across different regions and industries to minimize concentration risk.

6. Select Individual Investments:

Within each asset class, choose individual investments. For stocks, this may include selecting a mix of large-cap and small-cap stocks. For bonds, consider government, corporate, and municipal bonds.

7. **Utilize Mutual Funds and ETFs:**

Mutual funds and exchange-traded funds (ETFs) offer instant diversification by pooling assets across various securities. Choose funds that align with your investment strategy and goals.

8. **Rebalance Regularly:**

Periodically rebalance your portfolio to maintain the desired asset allocation. Market fluctuations may lead to deviations from the original plan, and rebalancing ensures alignment with your goals.

9. **Consider Risk Factors:**

Assess and manage specific risk factors. Evaluate factors like interest rate risk, credit risk, and market risk to make informed decisions about the composition of your portfolio.

10. **Factor in Liquidity Needs:**

Consider your liquidity needs when building your portfolio. Ensure that you have enough liquid assets to cover short-term expenses and emergencies without disrupting long-term investments.

11. Monitor Economic Conditions:

Stay informed about economic conditions and market trends. Economic changes may impact different asset classes differently, and a proactive approach helps you make timely adjustments.

12. Diversify Within Asset Classes:

Within each asset class, diversify further. For stocks, consider diversifying by industry, market capitalization, and geographic location. For bonds, diversify by issuer and maturity.

13. Evaluate Tax Implications:

Understand the tax implications of your investment decisions. Utilize tax-advantaged accounts, such as IRAs or 401(k)s, and consider the tax efficiency of your investment strategy.

14. Consider Alternative Investments:

Explore alternative investments, such as real estate, precious metals, or private equity, to further diversify your portfolio. Alternative investments can offer unique risk-return profiles.

15. Seek Professional Advice:

If needed, seek advice from financial professionals. A financial advisor can provide insights into building a diversified portfolio based on your specific financial situation and goals.

16. Stay Disciplined:

Maintain discipline in sticking to your investment plan. Avoid emotional reactions to short-term market fluctuations, and make decisions based on your long-term goals.

17. Periodic Review and Adjustment:

Regularly review your portfolio and assess its performance against your goals. Adjustments may be necessary based on changes in your financial situation or market conditions.

18. Reassess as Goals Evolve:

As your financial goals evolve, reassess and adjust your portfolio. Life events such as marriage, the birth of a child, or changes in income may warrant modifications to your investment strategy.

Creating a diversified investment portfolio is an ongoing process that requires attention, analysis, and adaptability. By following these steps and considering your unique circumstances, you can build a portfolio that aligns with your financial goals and withstands the challenges of the market. Remember, diversification is a key principle for managing risk and optimizing returns in the dynamic world of investing.

CHAPTER 4: TACKLING DEBT HEAD-ON

Welcome to a chapter that marks a decisive step towards financial liberation – "Tackling Debt Head-On." In the complex landscape of personal finance, the burden of debt can cast a shadow over your aspirations and financial well-being. This chapter is your guide to confronting debt, empowering you with strategies, tools, and a mindset that will propel you towards a debt-free future.

Debt is a common companion on life's journey, manifesting in various forms such as credit card balances, student loans, mortgages, and personal loans. While it may feel overwhelming, it's crucial to remember that you hold the power to shape your financial destiny. "Tackling Debt Head-On" is not just about repayment; it's a transformative journey that involves understanding, planning, and making deliberate choices to regain control of your financial narrative.

In the following pages, we delve into the roots of debt, exploring the psychological and practical aspects that contribute to its presence in our lives. From creating a comprehensive debt repayment strategy to cultivating habits that prevent future debt accumulation, this chapter provides a roadmap for overcoming the challenges posed by indebtedness.

We recognize that each debt journey is unique, and there's no one-size-fits-all solution. Whether you're dealing with overwhelming credit card balances, student loans, or a mortgage, this chapter offers tailored advice and actionable steps to address your specific circumstances.

As you embark on the journey of "Tackling Debt Head-On," envision it as a process of liberation – a pathway towards financial freedom unencumbered by the weight of debt. By embracing the principles outlined in this chapter, you're taking the first steps towards a brighter financial future. It's time to face debt with determination, resilience, and a commitment to reclaiming control over your financial destiny. Let's embark on this empowering journey together, where every effort brings you closer to a life unburdened by debt and filled with financial confidence.

- Identifying and Prioritizing Debts

Confronting and managing debt is a crucial step toward achieving financial well-being. To navigate the path to debt freedom effectively, it's essential to identify and prioritize your debts. This comprehensive guide explores the step-by-step process of recognizing and organizing your debts, empowering you to create a strategic repayment plan.

1. **Gather Debt Information:**

Begin by compiling a comprehensive list of all your debts. Include credit card balances, student loans, mortgages, personal loans, and any other outstanding obligations. Gather information on interest rates, minimum payments, and due dates.

2. Check Credit Reports:

Obtain your credit reports from major credit bureaus. Reviewing these reports helps ensure that you haven't overlooked any debts. It also provides insights into your overall credit health.

3. Categorize Debts:

Categorize your debts based on their type, interest rate, and purpose. Common categories include high-interest debts (credit cards), lower-interest debts (student loans), and secured debts (mortgages or car loans).

4. Determine Outstanding Balances:

Calculate the total outstanding balance for each debt category. This gives you a clear picture of the overall debt load and is a starting point for creating a repayment plan.

5. **Note Interest Rates:**

Take note of the interest rates associated with each debt. High-interest debts typically cost more over time, so prioritizing them can be financially advantageous.

6. **Assess Repayment Terms:**

Understand the repayment terms for each debt. Some may have fixed monthly payments, while others may offer flexibility. Knowing these terms helps in crafting a realistic repayment strategy.

7. **Evaluate Minimum Payments:**

Identify the minimum monthly payments required for each debt. Ensuring that you meet these minimums prevents late fees and protects your credit score.

8. **Consider Tax Implications:**

Be aware of any tax implications related to your debts. For example, mortgage interest may be tax-deductible, influencing your prioritization strategy.

9. Prioritize Based on Interest Rates:

Prioritize debts based on their interest rates. High-interest debts should often be tackled first to minimize overall interest payments.

10. Consider Emotional Impact:

Assess the emotional impact of each debt. While interest rates are crucial, paying off smaller debts first (the snowball method) can provide psychological wins, motivating you to tackle larger debts.

11. Evaluate Secured vs. Unsecured Debts:

Distinguish between secured and unsecured debts. Secured debts are backed by collateral (e.g., a home or car). Failing to repay them can result in the loss of assets, making them a priority.

12. Assess Financial Impact:

Evaluate the financial impact of each debt's elimination. Some debts, when paid off, free up significant monthly cash flow, allowing for faster repayment of other obligations.

13. **Create a Debt Repayment Plan:**

Based on your assessments, create a detailed debt repayment plan. Outline monthly payments, due dates, and the order in which you'll tackle each debt.

14. **Explore Debt Consolidation Options:**

Investigate debt consolidation options, such as balance transfer credit cards or consolidation loans. Consolidation can simplify payments and potentially lower interest rates.

15. **Negotiate with Creditors:**

If facing financial hardship, consider negotiating with creditors. Some may be willing to adjust interest rates, offer hardship plans, or settle for a reduced amount.

16. **Allocate Windfalls and Bonuses:**

Strategically allocate windfalls, tax refunds, or work bonuses toward debt repayment. This accelerates your progress without affecting your regular budget.

17. Automate Payments:

Set up automatic payments for minimum amounts to ensure on-time payments. This prevents late fees and protects your credit score.

18. Regularly Review and Adjust:

Periodically review your debt repayment plan and adjust as needed. Life circumstances and financial goals may change, requiring modifications to your strategy.

19. Celebrate Milestones:

Acknowledge and celebrate milestones along the way. Whether it's paying off a credit card or reaching a specific debt reduction goal, celebrating achievements reinforces positive financial habits.

By systematically identifying and prioritizing your debts, you lay the foundation for a successful debt repayment journey. Remember, the goal is not just to eliminate debts but to cultivate lasting financial habits that support your overall well-being. Approach this process with determination, discipline, and the knowledge that each step brings you closer to financial freedom.

- Strategies for Effective Debt Management

Effectively managing debt is a key component of achieving financial well-being and stability. Whether facing credit card balances, student loans, or other obligations, implementing strategic debt management techniques can alleviate financial stress and pave the way to debt freedom. In this comprehensive guide, we explore proven strategies to empower you in the journey towards effective debt management.

1. **Create a Detailed Budget:**

Begin by establishing a comprehensive budget that outlines your income, expenses, and debt obligations. A budget provides a clear understanding of your financial situation and serves as the foundation for effective debt management.

2. **Prioritize High-Interest Debts:**

Prioritize debts with the highest interest rates. Paying off high-interest debts first minimizes the overall interest you'll pay over time, accelerating your journey to debt freedom.

3. **Utilize the Snowball Method:**

Consider the snowball method, which involves paying off the smallest debts first. While this may not optimize interest savings, it provides psychological wins and motivation as smaller debts are eliminated.

4. **Consolidate Debts:**

Explore debt consolidation options, such as balance transfer credit cards or consolidation loans. Consolidating multiple debts into a single, lower-interest account can simplify payments and reduce overall interest costs.

5. Negotiate Interest Rates:

Negotiate with creditors for lower interest rates, especially if you have a good payment history. A reduced interest rate can significantly decrease the total amount you repay.

6. Avoid Adding New Debt:

Commit to not accumulating new debt while working on repayment. Focus on addressing existing obligations before taking on additional financial responsibilities.

7. Build an Emergency Fund:

Establish and maintain an emergency fund to cover unexpected expenses. Having a financial cushion prevents reliance on credit cards or loans during emergencies, aiding in debt avoidance.

8. Increase Income:

Explore opportunities to increase your income, such as seeking a higher-paying job, taking on a side gig, or monetizing skills and talents. Extra income can be directed towards debt repayment.

9. Allocate Windfalls Toward Debt:

Allocate unexpected windfalls, such as tax refunds or work bonuses, toward debt repayment. Using these financial boosts strategically accelerates your progress.

10. Set Realistic Goals:

Establish realistic and achievable debt repayment goals. Break down large debts into manageable milestones, celebrating achievements along the way to maintain motivation.

11. Automate Payments:

Set up automatic payments for at least the minimum amounts due on your debts. This ensures timely payments, prevents late fees, and protects your credit score.

12. Seek Professional Advice:

If your debt situation is complex, consider seeking advice from financial professionals. Credit counsellors or financial advisors can provide personalized strategies and assistance in negotiating with creditors.

13. Sell Unnecessary Assets:

Consider selling assets you no longer need to generate extra funds for debt repayment. This can include unused items, a second car, or other non-essential possessions.

14. Cut Discretionary Spending:

Identify and cut discretionary spending to free up more funds for debt repayment. Evaluate non-essential expenses and prioritize necessities while on the journey to debt freedom.

15. Track Your Progress:

Regularly monitor your progress toward debt reduction. Tracking your success reinforces positive financial habits and allows for adjustments to your strategy as needed.

16. Educate Yourself:

Invest time in financial education to enhance your understanding of debt management strategies, budgeting, and overall personal finance. Knowledge empowers informed decision-making.

17. Consider Debt Settlement:

As a last resort, explore debt settlement options if you are facing severe financial hardship. Debt settlement involves negotiating with creditors to settle for a reduced amount, but it can impact your credit score.

18. Stay Disciplined:

Maintain discipline throughout the debt management process. Avoid impulsive spending, adhere to your budget, and stay focused on your financial goals.

19. Celebrate Achievements:

Celebrate milestones and achievements in your debt repayment journey. Recognizing your progress boosts morale and reinforces the positive financial behaviors you've developed.

Effectively managing debt requires a combination of financial discipline, strategic planning, and a commitment to long-term financial well-being. By implementing these strategies, you equip yourself with the tools necessary to overcome debt challenges and work towards a future of financial freedom. Remember, each step you take brings you closer to a life unburdened by debt and filled with financial confidence.

- Eliminating Debt and Building Credit

Eliminating debt and building credit are intertwined components of achieving financial health and independence. This comprehensive guide outlines a strategic process to help you navigate the journey of becoming debt-free while simultaneously enhancing your credit profile.

1. Assess Your Debt Situation:

Begin by conducting a thorough assessment of your current debt. Compile a list of all outstanding balances, interest rates, and minimum monthly payments. Understanding the extent of your debt is the first step toward effective elimination.

2. Create a Realistic Repayment Plan:

Develop a comprehensive debt repayment plan that aligns with your budget and financial goals.

Prioritize debts based on interest rates, focusing on high-interest obligations first. Establish realistic timelines for repayment.

3. **Consolidate High-Interest Debts:**

Explore debt consolidation options, such as balance transfer credit cards or consolidation loans. Consolidating high-interest debts into a single, lower-interest account can streamline payments and reduce overall interest costs.

4. **Negotiate with Creditors:**

Engage in open communication with creditors to negotiate lower interest rates or more favorable repayment terms. Many creditors are willing to work with individuals facing financial challenges, especially if it ensures repayment.

5. **Leverage Windfalls and Bonuses:**

Allocate unexpected windfalls, tax refunds, or work bonuses toward debt repayment. Utilizing unexpected financial gains strategically accelerates the debt-elimination process.

6. Automate Payments:

Set up automatic payments for at least the minimum amounts due on your debts. This ensures on-time payments, preventing late fees, and is a positive factor for your credit score.

7. Maintain Emergency Savings:

Build and maintain an emergency fund to cover unforeseen expenses without resorting to additional debt. Having a financial safety net promotes responsible financial management.

8. Increase Income:

Seek opportunities to increase your income, whether through a side job, freelance work, or career advancement. Supplementing your income can provide additional resources for debt repayment.

9. Review and Adjust:

Regularly review your debt repayment plan and make adjustments as needed. Life circumstances and financial goals may change, necessitating modifications to your strategy.

10. Understand Credit Report and Score:

Familiarize yourself with your credit report and credit score. Understand the factors that influence your score, such as payment history, credit utilization, length of credit history, types of credit, and new credit.

11. Dispute Inaccuracies on Credit Report:

Check your credit report for inaccuracies and dispute any discrepancies you find. Correcting inaccuracies ensures that your credit report accurately reflects your financial history.

12. Limit New Credit Applications:

Limit the number of new credit applications to avoid inquiries that can slightly impact your credit score. Opening multiple new accounts within a short period may be perceived as a higher risk.

13. Diversify Types of Credit:

Maintain a mix of different types of credit, such as credit cards, instalment loans, and retail accounts. A diversified credit portfolio positively influences your credit score.

14. Keep Credit Card Balances Low:

Aim to keep credit card balances low relative to your credit limit. High credit utilization can negatively impact your credit score. Strive to use no more than 30% of your available credit.

15. Establish Good Payment Habits:

Consistently make on-time payments for all your credit obligations. Timely payments contribute significantly to a positive credit history and demonstrate financial responsibility.

16. **Limit Closing Old Accounts:**

Avoid closing old credit accounts, as the length of your credit history is a factor in your credit score. Closing old accounts can shorten your credit history and potentially affect your score.

17. **Seek Secured Credit Options:**

If needed, explore secured credit card options to build or rebuild credit. Secured cards require a security deposit but can be instrumental in establishing a positive credit history.

18. **Patiently Rebuild Credit:**

Recognize that rebuilding credit is a gradual process. Patience and consistent positive financial behavior are key elements in enhancing your credit profile over time.

19. **Monitor Your Progress:**

Regularly monitor your debt reduction progress and credit score. Tracking improvements in both areas reinforces positive financial habits and motivates continued responsible financial management.

By systematically addressing your debt and building a positive credit history, you empower yourself with financial stability and open doors to future opportunities. Remember, the journey to financial well-being is a gradual process, and each step you take brings you closer to a life free from the burden of debt and filled with creditworthiness.

CHAPTER 5: GENERATING SUSTAINABLE INCOME STREAMS

Welcome to the transformative chapter on "Generating Sustainable Income Streams." In the dynamic landscape of personal finance, the ability to create consistent and sustainable sources of income is a cornerstone of financial independence. This chapter serves as your comprehensive guide, unveiling strategies and insights to diversify and fortify your income streams, empowering you to build a resilient and prosperous financial future.

In an ever-evolving economic environment, the traditional concept of relying solely on a single income source is increasingly viewed as a precarious approach. "Generating Sustainable Income Streams" is not just about making money;

it's about adopting a mindset that embraces diversity, resilience, and innovation in your pursuit of financial stability.

Throughout this chapter, we explore a myriad of income-generating avenues, from traditional employment to entrepreneurial endeavors, investments, and passive income streams. Whether you're looking to augment your current income, embark on a new career path, or secure your financial future, the strategies outlined here are designed to suit various aspirations and circumstances.

The journey towards sustainable income involves not only practical strategies but also a mindset shift—a realization that financial success is attainable through creativity, adaptability, and strategic planning. As we delve into the strategies and tactics presented in this chapter, consider them as building blocks for constructing a robust financial foundation—one that withstands economic fluctuations and empowers you to achieve your life goals.

So, whether you're seeking financial freedom, planning for retirement, or aiming to fulfil personal aspirations, "Generating Sustainable Income Streams" is your roadmap to navigating the diverse landscape of income generation. Prepare to explore new possibilities, harness your skills and talents, and embark on a journey that transcends the boundaries of conventional financial thinking. Your financial future is in your hands, and this chapter is your guide to unlocking the potential of sustainable income streams. Let's begin the transformative exploration of diversified and resilient income generation together.

- Multiple Income Sources

In the dynamic landscape of personal finance, relying on a single income source may not provide the financial security and flexibility needed to navigate life's uncertainties. Diversifying income streams has become a crucial strategy for building resilience, achieving financial goals, and ensuring long-term stability. This comprehensive guide explores the concept of multiple income sources, offering insights into various avenues for generating revenue.

1. Traditional Employment:

- **Description:** Traditional employment remains a fundamental source of income. Full-time, part-time, or contract work provides a consistent paycheck and often includes benefits such as health insurance and retirement plans.

- **Pros:** Stability, benefits, and a predictable income stream.

- **Cons:** Limited flexibility, dependence on a single employer.

2. Freelancing and Consulting:

- Description: Freelancing or consulting allows individuals to offer their skills and services on a project basis. This can include writing, graphic design, marketing, IT services, and more.

   - **Pros:** Flexibility, potential for higher income rates, and the ability to choose clients and projects.

   - **Cons:** Variable income, lack of job security.

3. Side Hustles:

   - **Description:** Side hustles are part-time endeavors pursued alongside a primary job. This could involve selling products online, offering services, or monetizing a hobby or passion.

   - **Pros:** Additional income, potential for growth into a full-time venture, and flexibility.

   - **Cons:** Balancing multiple commitments, the potential for burnout.

4. Investment Income:

   - **Description:** Investment income comes from returns on invested capital. This can include dividends from stocks, interest from bonds, and capital gains from the sale of assets.

- **Pros:** Passive income, potential for capital appreciation.

- **Cons:** Market risks, initial capital required.

5. **Real Estate:**

- **Description:** Real estate can generate income through rental properties or property appreciation. This includes residential and commercial real estate investments.

- **Pros:** Monthly rental income, potential for property value appreciation.

- **Cons:** Property management responsibilities, market fluctuations.

6. **Business Ownership:**

- **Description:** Owning a business, whether small or large, provides opportunities for income generation. This could be a retail store, an online venture, or a franchise.

- **Pros:** Entrepreneurial freedom, the potential for substantial profits.

- **Cons:** Business risks, time-intensive, initial capital and effort required.

7. Passive Income Streams:

- **Description:** Passive income requires minimal effort to maintain. Examples include royalties from intellectual property, affiliate marketing, or income from automated online businesses.

- **Pros:** Minimal time commitment, potential for continuous income.

- **Cons:** Initial effort and time required to set up, potential for lower initial returns.

8. Dividend Income:

- **Description:** Dividend income is earned by holding stocks that pay regular dividends. This provides a share in the company's profits.

- **Pros:** Regular income, potential for reinvestment and compounding.

- **Cons:** Market risks, dependent on company performance.

9. Educational Products and Courses:

- **Description:** Creating and selling educational products, courses, or e-books allows individuals to monetize their expertise.

- **Pros:** Scalable income, potential for passive earnings.

- **Cons:** Initial effort required to create content and marketing challenges.

10. Royalties:

- **Description:** Royalties are payments received for the use of intellectual property, such as books, music, or patents.

- **Pros:** Passive income, potential for long-term revenue.

- **Cons:** Initial effort in creating intellectual property, market changes.

11. **Network Marketing or Multi-Level Marketing (MLM):**

- **Description:** MLM involves earning commissions not only from personal sales but also from the sales of a recruited team. Products or services are typically sold through a network.

- **Pros:** Potential for unlimited earning, and flexibility.

- **Cons:** Controversial business model, potential for high competition.

12. **Online Platforms and Content Creation:**

- **Description:** Content creation on platforms like YouTube, podcasts, or blogs can generate income through ads, sponsorships, and merchandise sales.

- **Pros:** Creative expression, the potential for a wide reach.

- **Cons:** Time-consuming, competitive landscape.

13. Government Assistance or Social Security:

- **Description:** Government assistance programs or social security can serve as a supplementary income source, particularly during retirement.

- **Pros:** Guaranteed income, and financial support.

- **Cons:** Eligibility requirements, potential limitations.

14. License Your Photography or Art:

- **Description:** Licensing your creative work allows others to use it for a fee. This can apply to photography, artwork, or designs.

- **Pros:** Passive income, potential for exposure.

- **Cons:** Need for high-quality, marketable creations.

15. Teaching or Tutoring:

- **Description**: Providing educational services as a tutor or instructor can be done online or in person.

- **Pros:** Flexibility, opportunity to share expertise.

- **Cons:** Time-intensive, potentially variable income.

16. **Peer-to-Peer Lending:**

- **Description:** Peer-to-peer lending platforms allow individuals to lend money directly to others in exchange for interest payments.

- **Pros:** Passive income, potential for higher returns than traditional savings.

- **Cons:** Risk of borrower default, market changes.

17. **Affiliate Marketing:**

- **Description:** Affiliate marketing involves earning a commission by promoting other companies' products or services.

- **Pros:** Passive income, no need to create products.

- **Cons:** Market saturation, dependence on affiliate programs.

18. **Participate in Clinical Trials or Research Studies:**

- **Description:** Participating in clinical trials or research studies can provide compensation.

- **Pros:** Potential for supplemental income, and contribution to research.

- **Cons:** Eligibility criteria, potential risks.

19. **Online Surveys and Market Research:**

- **Description:** Participating in online surveys or market research can result in small payments or gift cards.

- **Pros:** Easy to participate, minimal time commitment.

- **Cons:** Low individual payouts, time-consuming for significant earnings.

20. Create and Sell Handmade Products:

- **Description:** Crafting handmade products and selling them on platforms like Etsy can be a source of income.

- **Pros:** Creative expression, the potential for scalability.

- **Cons:** Time-intensive, market competition.

21. Virtual Assistance:

- **Description:** Providing virtual assistance services, such as administrative support, to businesses or entrepreneurs.

- **Pros:** Flexibility, potential for remote work.

- **Cons:** Time constraints, need for specific skills.

22. Rent Out Assets:

- **Description:** Renting out assets like a room on Airbnb, a car, or equipment can generate extra income.

- **Pros:** Utilizing existing assets, potential for passive income.

- **Cons**: Initial setup, potential maintenance.

23. **Sell Stock Photography:**

- **Description:** Selling high-quality photos to stock photography platforms can generate income through licensing.

- **Pros:** Passive income, potential for widespread usage.

- **Cons:** Need for high-quality, marketable photos.

24. **Remote Work or Telecommuting:**

- **Description:** Remote work involves performing a job from a location other than the employer's office. This can be full-time or part-time.

- **Pros:** Flexibility, potential for diverse opportunities.

- **Cons:** Dependency on internet connectivity, potential for isolation.

25. **Participate in the Gig Economy:**

- **Description:** Participating in the gig economy by offering services through platforms like Uber, Lyft, or TaskRabbit.

- **Pros:** Flexibility, on-demand opportunities.

- Cons: Variable income, lack of job security.

26. **Create and Sell Online Courses:**

- **Description:** Creating and selling online courses on platforms like Udemy or Teachable.

- **Pros:** Passive income, scalable.

- **Cons:** Initial effort in course creation, market competition.

27. Write and Self-Publish Books:

- **Description:** Writing and self-publishing books, whether fiction or non-fiction, can be a source of royalty income.

- **Pros:** Creative expression, potential for passive income.

- **Cons:** Initial effort in writing and publishing, market competition.

28. Create and Sell Software:

- **Description:** Developing and selling software applications or tools.

- **Pros:** Potential for substantial profits, scalability.

- **Cons:** Initial investment in development, competition.

29. Cryptocurrency Investments:

- **Description**: Investing in cryptocurrencies can potentially yield profits through price appreciation or staking.

   - **Pros:** Potential for high returns, 24/7 market.

   - **Cons**: Volatility, market risks.

30. **Create and Sell Art:**

   - **Description:** Selling original artwork, paintings, or sculptures either online or in galleries.

   - **Pros:** Creative expression, potential for unique revenue streams.

   - **Cons:** Market competition, subjective valuation.

Diversifying your income sources provides not only financial stability but also the flexibility to adapt to changing economic conditions. Consider your skills, interests, and risk tolerance when exploring these various avenues. Combining multiple income streams strategically can lead to a more robust and sustainable financial future. Whether you're aiming for financial independence, pursuing a passion, or simply seeking greater flexibility, the concept of multiple income sources is a dynamic and empowering approach to personal finance.

- Passive Income Strategies

Passive income strategies represent a paradigm shift in wealth creation, allowing individuals to earn money with minimal ongoing effort or active involvement. These strategies provide financial flexibility, create a buffer against economic uncertainties, and pave the way for a more secure financial future. This comprehensive guide explores various passive income strategies, elucidating their principles, advantages, and potential considerations.

1. **Dividend Stocks:**

 - **Description:** Investing in dividend-paying stocks provides a regular stream of income.

Companies distribute a portion of their profits to shareholders in the form of dividends.

- **Pros:** Regular income, potential for capital appreciation.

- **Cons:** Market risks, dependency on company performance.

2. Real Estate Investments:

- **Description:** Real estate, whether through rental properties or Real Estate Investment Trusts (REITs), generates passive income through rental payments or dividends.

- **Pros:** Monthly income, potential property appreciation.

- **Cons:** Property management responsibilities, market fluctuations.

3. Peer-to-Peer Lending:

- **Description:** Peer-to-peer lending platforms connect borrowers with individual lenders, allowing individuals to earn interest on loans.

- **Pros:** Passive income, potential for higher returns than traditional savings.

- **Cons:** Risk of borrower default, market changes.

4. Create and Sell Digital Products:

- **Description:** Creating and selling digital products such as e-books, online courses, or digital art allows for scalable passive income.

- **Pros:** Global reach, minimal ongoing effort.

- **Cons:** Initial effort in creation, market competition.

5. Dividend ETFs:

- **Description:** Dividend Exchange-Traded Funds (ETFs) pool investments in multiple dividend-paying stocks, providing investors with diversified income.

- **Pros:** Diversification, professional management.

- **Cons**: Market risks, management fees.

6. Automated Online Businesses:

- **Description:** Establishing automated online businesses, such as dropshipping, affiliate marketing, or niche websites, enables income generation with minimal ongoing involvement.

- **Pros:** Passive income, flexibility.

- **Cons:** Initial setup, competition.

7. Royalties from Intellectual Property:

- **Description:** Earning royalties from books, music, patents, or other intellectual property provides ongoing passive income.

- **Pros:** Potential for long-term revenue, passive nature.

- **Cons:** Initial effort in creation, market changes.

8. High-Yield Savings Accounts:

- **Description**: High-yield savings accounts offer higher interest rates than traditional savings accounts, generating passive income on deposited funds.

- **Pros:** Safety, liquidity.

- **Cons:** Lower interest rates in low-rate environments.

9. Affiliate Marketing:

- **Description:** Affiliate marketers earn commissions by promoting other companies' products or services, usually through blogs, websites, or social media.

- **Pros:** Passive income, no need to create products.

- **Cons:** Market saturation, dependence on affiliate programs.

10. Create and Sell Stock Photography:

- **Description:** Selling high-quality photos to stock photography platforms allows for passive income through licensing.

- **Pros:** Passive income, potential for widespread usage.

- **Cons:** Need for high-quality, marketable photos.

11. Create a Mobile App:

- **Description:** Developing and monetizing a mobile app can generate passive income through app purchases, ads, or in-app purchases.

- **Pros:** Scalability, potential for widespread use.

- **Cons:** Initial development costs, competition.

12. Invest in REITs:

- **Description**: Real Estate Investment Trusts (REITs) pool investments in real estate projects, providing investors with dividends from rental income.

- **Pros:** Diversification, professional management.

- **Cons**: Market risks, management fees.

13. **Create and Sell an Online Course:**

- **Description:** Creating and selling an online course on platforms like Udemy or Teachable allows for passive income through course enrollments.

- **Pros:** Scalable income, potential for passive earnings.

- **Cons:** Initial effort in course creation, and marketing challenges.

14. **High-Quality YouTube Channel:**

- **Description:** Building a high-quality YouTube channel with monetization enables creators to earn passive income through ad revenue and sponsorships.

- **Pros:** Scalability, global reach.

- **Cons:** Competitive landscape, initial effort.

15. Write and Self-Publish Books:

- **Description:** Writing and self-publishing books, whether fiction or non-fiction, can be a source of royalty income.

- **Pros:** Creative expression, potential for passive income.

- **Cons:** Initial effort in writing and publishing, market competition.

16. License Your Photography or Art:

- **Description:** Licensing your creative work allows others to use it for a fee. This can apply to photography, artwork, or designs.

- **Pros**: Passive income, potential for exposure.

- **Cons:** Need for high-quality, marketable creations.

17. Automated Dropshipping Business:

- **Description:** Dropshipping involves selling products without handling inventory. An automated dropshipping business allows for passive income through online sales.

   - **Pros:** Passive income, no inventory management.

   - Cons: Initial setup, market competition.

18. **Create and Sell Printable:**

   - **Description:** Designing and selling printable templates or digital products online can generate passive income through online marketplaces.

   - **Pros:** Scalability, minimal ongoing effort.

   - **Cons:** Initial design effort, market competition.

19. **Participate in Affiliate Programs:**

   - **Description:** Participating in affiliate programs for products or services relevant to your niche allows for passive income through referrals.

   - **Pros:** Passive income, no need to create products.

- **Cons:** Dependence on affiliate program policies.

20. Cryptocurrency Staking:

- **Description:** Staking involves locking up cryptocurrencies to support the operations of a blockchain network, earning passive income in the form of additional tokens.

- **Pros:** Potential for high returns, and participation in blockchain networks.

- Cons: Volatility, risks associated with specific cryptocurrencies.

21. Create and Sell Merchandise:

- **Description:** Designing and selling branded merchandise, such as T-shirts, mugs, or accessories, through print-on-demand services allows for passive income.

- **Pros:** Creative expression, minimal ongoing effort.

- **Cons:** Marketing challenges, competition.

22. **License Software or Technology:**

- **Description:** Licensing proprietary software or technology to other businesses or individuals allows for passive income through usage fees.

- **Pros:** Potential for continuous income, scalability.

- **Cons:** Intellectual property protection, market competition.

23. **Automated Niche Websites:**

- **Description:** Creating and monetizing niche websites with affiliate marketing, ads, or sponsored content enables passive income through website traffic.

- **Pros:** Passive income, potential for scalability

- **Cons:** Initial website setup, SEO challenges.

24. Participate in Automated Trading:

- **Description:** Automated trading involves using algorithms or trading bots to execute trades in financial markets, potentially generating passive income.

- **Pros:** Potential for returns, automated execution.

- **Cons:** Market risks, technical challenges.

25. Participate in Crowdfunding Projects:

- **Description:** Investing in crowdfunding projects, whether through equity crowdfunding or lending-based platforms, can yield passive income.

- **Pros:** Diversification, potential for returns.

- **Cons:** Risks associated with project success, lack of liquidity.

26. Rent Out Equipment or Tools:

- **Description:** Renting out equipment, tools, or assets to other individuals or businesses allows for passive income.

- **Pros:** Utilizing existing assets, potential for passive earnings.

- **Cons:** Maintenance and insurance considerations, market demand.

27. Automated Print-on-Demand Business:

- **Description:** Creating and selling custom-designed products through print-on-demand services enables passive income through online sales.

- **Pros:** Passive income, no inventory management.

- **Cons:** Initial setup, market competition.

28. Invest in Index Funds:

- **Description:** Investing in index funds, which track the performance of a market index, provides passive exposure to the overall market.

- **Pros:** Diversification, low fees.

- **Cons:** Market risks, lack of individual stock selection.

29. Rent Out Space on Your Property:

- **Description:** Renting out unused space on your property, whether as storage, parking, or event space, generates passive income.

- **Pros:** Utilizing existing space, potential for passive earnings.

- **Cons:** Property considerations, market demand.

30. Participate in Automated Affiliate Marketing:

- **Description:** Utilizing automated tools or platforms to manage and optimize affiliate marketing efforts for multiple products or services.

- **Pros:** Streamlined affiliate marketing, time-saving.

- **Cons**: Dependence on automation tools, the potential for errors.

Passive income strategies offer individuals the opportunity to break free from the limitations of traditional income models, creating financial independence and flexibility. While these strategies provide the potential for ongoing income with minimal effort, it's crucial to approach them with careful consideration, understand associated risks, and align them with your financial goals. Building a diversified portfolio of passive income streams can contribute to long-term financial stability and open the door to a more autonomous and fulfilling lifestyle.

- Building and Protecting Your Income Streams

Building and protecting your income streams are fundamental aspects of achieving financial stability and independence. This comprehensive guide explores strategies for diversifying and fortifying your income sources, ensuring resilience in the face of economic uncertainties, and creating a foundation for a secure financial future.

Building Your Income Streams:

1. **Diversification:**

   - **Description:** Diversifying your income sources is a key strategy to mitigate risks and create a more resilient financial portfolio. Explore various avenues such as employment, freelancing, investments, and entrepreneurship.

   - **Benefits**: Reduces dependency on a single source and increases financial flexibility.

2. Skill Development:

- **Description:** Continuously invest in developing new skills and enhancing existing ones. This not only makes you more versatile in the job market but also opens doors to new income-generating opportunities.

- **Benefits:** Increases earning potential, and adaptability to changing market demands.

3. Side Hustles and Entrepreneurship:

- **Description:** Explore side hustles or entrepreneurial ventures that align with your interests and skills. This could involve starting a small business, freelancing, or monetizing a hobby.

- **Benefits**: Additional income streams, the potential for long-term business success.

4. Investing:

- **Description:** Strategic investing in stocks, real estate, or other financial instruments can generate passive income and contribute to long-term wealth accumulation.

   - **Benefits:** Diversification, potential for capital appreciation.

5. Education and Certifications:

   - **Description:** Investing in education and certifications can enhance your qualifications, making you more competitive in your current job or opening doors to higher-paying opportunities.

   - **Benefits:** Career advancement, increased earning potential.

6. Building a Personal Brand:

   - **Description:** Cultivate a strong personal brand through online presence, networking, and showcasing your expertise. A well-established personal brand can attract opportunities and clients.

   - **Benefits:** Enhanced credibility, increased opportunities.

7. Multiple Income Streams:

- **Description:** Actively seek and create multiple income streams to create a robust financial portfolio. This could include a combination of active and passive sources.

- **Benefits:** Reduces financial risk and provides stability.

Protecting Your Income Streams:

1. Emergency Fund:

- **Description:** Establish and maintain an emergency fund that covers three to six months' worth of living expenses. This acts as a financial safety net during unexpected events.

- **Benefits:** Financial security, peace of mind.

2. Insurance:

- **Description:** Invest in insurance coverage such as health, life, disability, and income protection insurance. These safeguards provide financial support in times of illness, injury, or unforeseen circumstances.

   - **Benefits:** Financial protection, mitigates risks.

3. Diversification of Investments:

   - **Description:** Diversify your investment portfolio to spread risk. Avoid concentrating too much on one asset class or industry to minimize the impact of market fluctuations.

   - **Benefits:** Mitigates investment risk, and preserves wealth.

4. Continuous Learning and Adaptation:

   - **Description:** Stay informed about industry trends, economic changes, and technological advancements. Adaptability is key to navigating evolving markets and securing your income.

   - **Benefits:** Maintains competitiveness, and anticipates changes.

5. Debt Management:

- **Description:** Effectively manage and reduce high-interest debts. Develop a strategic plan to pay off outstanding debts, starting with those with the highest interest rates.

- **Benefits:** Reduces financial burden and improves cash flow.

6. Legal and Financial Planning:

- **Description:** Seek professional advice for legal and financial planning. This includes drafting wills, creating trusts, and ensuring your financial affairs are structured for optimal protection.

- **Benefits:** Asset protection, ensures legal clarity.

7. Regular Financial Checkups:

- **Description:** Conduct regular assessments of your financial health. Review your income, expenses, investments, and overall financial goals to make informed decisions.

- **Benefits:** Identifies areas for improvement, and ensures financial well-being.

8. Budgeting:

- **Description:** Develop and stick to a comprehensive budget. Tracking your income and expenses provides a clear overview of your financial situation, enabling informed decision-making.

- **Benefits:** Financial discipline, prevents overspending.

9. Negotiation Skills:

- **Description:** Hone your negotiation skills, whether in salary negotiations, business deals, or contract discussions. Maximize your earning potential by advocating for fair compensation.

- **Benefits**: Increased income, better financial terms.

10. Cybersecurity:

- **Description:** Safeguard your online presence and financial accounts against cyber threats. Use strong passwords, enable two-factor authentication, and stay vigilant against phishing attempts.

- **Benefits:** Protects financial assets, and prevents identity theft.

11. Crisis Planning:

- **Description:** Develop a crisis plan for unexpected events such as job loss, economic downturns, or health crises. Having a plan in place can ease financial stress during challenging times.

- **Benefits:** Preparedness reduces panic.

12. Networking:

- **Description:** Cultivate a strong professional network. Networking can open doors to new opportunities, collaborations, and potential income streams.

- **Benefits**: Access to opportunities, and career support.

13. Continuous Professional Development:

- **Description:** Invest in continuous learning and professional development to stay relevant in your industry. This enhances job security and opens avenues for career advancement.

- **Benefits:** Career growth, increased income potential.

14. **Tax Planning:**

- **Description:** Implement effective tax planning strategies to optimize your tax liabilities. Utilize available deductions and credits to maximize your take-home income.

- **Benefits:** Maximizes income, and reduces tax burden.

Building and protecting your income streams requires a proactive and strategic approach. By diversifying your income sources, implementing risk-mitigating measures, and staying attuned to changes in the financial landscape, you can create a solid foundation for financial success. Remember that financial well-being is an ongoing journey, and

regularly reassessing and adjusting your strategies
will contribute to long-term stability and prosperity.

CONCUSION

As we conclude "The Financial Freedom Formula: A Step-by-Step Guide to Financial Independence," I want to express my gratitude for joining me on this transformative journey. We've navigated the intricate terrain of personal finance, unravelling the threads that weave together the fabric of financial independence. The insights shared within these pages are not just theoretical concepts but actionable steps that, when embraced, can lead you to a future defined by freedom, security, and abundance.

In our exploration, we've dissected the essence of financial freedom, understanding its nuanced components and uncovering the importance of each pillar in the formula. From assessing your current financial situation to setting realistic goals, crafting a personalized budget, and mastering the art of investing, we've left no stone unturned. Tackling debt head-on, generating sustainable income streams, and building emergency funds for stability were not mere topics but crucial milestones on your path to economic liberation.

Throughout these chapters, you've been equipped with tools to assess, plan, and take decisive actions toward your financial goals. We've delved into the intricacies of multiple income sources, passive income strategies, and the art of protecting and diversifying your financial assets. The journey toward financial independence is not a sprint but a marathon, requiring consistency, adaptability, and a commitment to lifelong learning.

Remember, the financial freedom formula is not a one-size-fits-all prescription. It's a guide, a compass that empowers you to chart your unique course. Your financial journey is as individual as your fingerprint, and the strategies presented here are the stepping stones, not the destination.

As you embark on applying these principles to your life, stay resilient in the face of challenges, stay disciplined in your financial habits, and stay committed to the vision of the life you aspire to lead. Financial freedom is not just about accumulating wealth; it's about gaining control over your choices, having the ability to pursue your passions, and creating a life that aligns with your values.

In closing, I challenge you to envision the life you desire, armed with the knowledge and tools you've acquired. May the Financial Freedom Formula serve as your compass, guiding you through the twists and turns of your financial journey? Here's to your prosperity, your freedom, and the limitless possibilities that await on the road to financial independence. May your financial future be a testament to the power of deliberate choices and the pursuit of a life well-lived?